W9-AKE-255

Inventions and Discoveries

The Arts

WORLD BOOK

a Scott Fetzer company

Chicago

www.worldbookonline.com

World Book, Inc.
233 N. Michigan Avenue
Chicago, IL 60601
U.S.A.

For information about other World Book publications, visit our Web site at **http://www.worldbookonline.com** or call **1-800-WORLDBK (967-5325)**.
For information about sales to schools and libraries, call **1-800-975-3250 (United States)**, or **1-800-837-5365 (Canada)**.

Editorial:
Editor in Chief: Paul A. Kobasa
Project Manager: Cassie Mayer
Editor: Jake Bumgardner
Content Development: Odyssey Books
Writer: Anna-Maria Crum
Researcher: Cheryl Graham
Manager, Contracts & Compliance
  (Rights & Permissions): Loranne K. Shields
Indexer: David Pofelski

Graphics and Design:
Associate Director: Sandra M. Dyrlund
Manager, Graphics and Design: Tom Evans
Coordinator, Design Development and Production:
  Brenda B. Tropinski
Senior Designer: Don Di Sante
Contributing Photographs Editor: Clover Morell

Pre-Press and Manufacturing:
Director: Carma Fazio
Manufacturing Manager: Steven K. Hueppchen
Production/Technology Manager: Anne Fritzinger

Picture Acknowledgments:

Front Cover: © iRepublic/Masterfile; Back Cover: Bridgeman Art Library.

© Alamy Images 7; © Marion Kaplan, Alamy Images 4; © London Art Archive/Alamy Images 6; © Print Collector/Alamy Images 11, 31; © Real World People/Alamy Images 15; © shinypix/Alamy Images 21; © Jupiter Images/Thinkstock /Alamy Images 23; © Elizabeth Whiting & Associates/Alamy Images 13; © Darrell Young, Alamy Images 41; AP/Wide World 22, 43; © British Museum/Art Resource 5; © DeA Picture Library/Art Resource 24; © Erich Lessing, Art Resource 5, 37; *Annunciation* (detail of Gabriel) by Simone Martini; Uffizi, Florence, Italy (Erich Lessing, Art Resource) 25; *The Dance* (1988), acrylic on paper laid on canvas by Paula Rego; Tate, London (Art Resource) 29; Bridgeman Art Library 9, 33; © Archives Charmet/Bridgeman Art Library 18; © Conservatoire National des Arts et Metiers/ Bridgeman Art Library 38; © Ham House/ Bridgeman Art Library 10; *The Starry Night* (1889), oil on canvas by Vincent van Gogh; Museum of Modern Art, New York (Bridgeman Art Library) 27; *The Arnolfini Marriage* (1434), oil on panel by Jan van Eyck; National Gallery, London, UK (Bridgeman Art Library) 27; © The Stapleton Collection/Bridgeman Art Library 18; © Corbis/ Bettmann 37, 39, 41; © Ethel Davies, Corbis 9; © Henry Diltz, Corbis 15; © Owen Franken, Corbis 5; © Michael Freeman, Corbis 32; © Hulton-Deutsch Collection/Corbis 33; © David Lees, Corbis 30; © Gabe Palmer, Corbis 26; © Schenectady Museum/Corbis 40; © TW-Photo/Corbis 39; © Patrick Ward, Corbis 8; Don Di Sante 32; Eastman Kodak 41; George Eastman House 35; © Getty Images 29; © David Allan Brandt, Getty Images 13; © Dorling Kindersley/Getty Images 11; © Hulton Archive/Getty Images 14; © Bob Thomas, Getty Images 17; © Time & Life Pictures/Getty Images 36; Granger Collection 12, 16, 17, 19, 35, 38; Library of Congress 34; © Peter Byron, PhotoEdit 42; © Jeff Greenberg, PhotoEdit 28; © David Young-Wolff, PhotoEdit 43; © Shutterstock 25, 44.

All maps and illustrations are the exclusive property of World Book, Inc.

Library of Congress Cataloging-in-Publication Data

The arts.
    p. cm. – (Inventions and discoveries)
  Includes index.
  Summary: "An exploration of the transformative impact of inventions and discoveries in the arts. Features include fact boxes, sidebars, biographies, timeline, glossary, list of recommended reading and Web sites, and index"–Provided by publisher.
  ISBN 978-0-7166-0383-2
  1. Technology and the arts–Juvenile literature. 2. Arts–Technological innovations--Juvenile literature. I. World Book, Inc.
  NX180.T4A789 2009
  700'.1'05–dc22
                        2008042560

Inventions and Discoveries
Set ISBN: 978-0-7166-0380-1
Printed in China
1 2 3 4 5 12 11 10 09

▶ Table of Contents

There is a glossary of terms on pages 45-46. Terms defined in the glossary are in type **that looks like this** on their first appearance on any spread (two facing pages).

Art comes in many colors, styles, and forms. Rodolfo Morales, a Mexican artist, used bright colors in his paintings.

What is an invention?

An invention is a new device, new product, or new way of doing something. Inventions change the way people live. Before the car was invented, some people rode horses to travel long distances. Before the light bulb was invented, people used candles and similar sources of light to see at night. Today, inventions continue to change the way we live.

What are the arts?

The word *art* can be used in many different ways. There are useful arts, which produce objects for everyday use, like a ceramic bowl. And there are decorative arts, which produce beautiful objects for their own sake, like jewelry. Performing arts include drama, music, and dance. **Fine arts** include things like painting, writing novels, acting, or playing and composing music. Today, some works of architecture, moviemaking, **photography,** pottery, and weaving, and some forms of modern dance are also considered fine arts.

Works of fine art can differ in several ways. They may tell a story and take time to unfold, as in a novel or a play. Or they may be presented all at once, as with a painting. Some forms of art, like sculpture, may be completed single-handedly by the artist. Others must be performed by actors or musicians.

Some arts date back to prehistoric times. Prehistoric people probably created the first musical rhythms by stomping their feet and clapping their hands. The first musical instruments may have been bones, rocks, or hunting tools that were struck against each other to create a rhythmic beat.

Ancient people made many types of musical instruments, such as bone flutes (left) and wooden slit-drums (below).

Prehistoric people used dances and paintings to communicate the idea of success in planting, harvesting, and hunting. The ancient Greeks made beautiful statues of gods and goddesses to express such human qualities as wisdom and courage.

As different **civilizations** came into contact with one another, they shared their knowledge of the arts. Artistic objects were passed along, such as musical instruments, as were artistic techniques, such as certain styles of painting.

Over time, artists and inventors developed new musical instruments, new ways of painting, and new technologies that have created new forms of art. Many inventions develop slowly over time, such as methods of painting or playing music. Others developed rapidly, such as the invention of **motion pictures.**

The arts continue to play an important role in people's lives. Through the arts, people explore the meaning of important events in their lives and share these experiences with others.

Making music seems to be a basic part of human nature. This jazz band plays on a bridge in Paris, France.

Playing Music: The Keyboard

▶ The Organ

This ancient Roman organist performs with a horn player at a festival.

Most musical instruments have their beginnings in the earliest **civilizations.** Many instruments have changed over time. People adapted changes from other technologies to musical instruments to make them easier to play or to make better sounds. The shape or size of some instruments was changed so they would make more or different sounds. Keyboard instruments are an example of how early musical instruments evolved into the musical instruments we use today.

One of the earliest forms of a keyboard instrument is the **organ.** The organ dates back to the 200's B.C., when an **engineer** in ancient Greece named Ctesibius (*tee SIHB ee uhs*) designed the hydraulis (*hy DRAW luhs*). This organ used water power to force air into the organ's pipes. The vibration of the air inside the pipes produced the organ's sound. At first, the organ included only one row of pipes and just a few keys. Later designs of the organ included many rows of pipes.

The hydraulis was used for many occasions, including banquets, theater performances, and arena events. However, the instrument needed constant maintenance. Water caused parts of the organ to become corroded (worn away) easily.

By the A.D. 200's, engineers developed an organ that used a windbag instead of a water tank. The windbag organ design included bellows, devices that produce wind by sucking air through one or more valves and then pumping it out.

The major features of the modern organ were developed between the 200's and 1500's. By the end of the 1400's, organs looked much like they do today, with many rows of pipes and a full keyboard.

Cathedral organs, like this one in Rome, Italy, are sometimes so big that they are built as part of the church.

From the 1500's to the mid-1700's, many composers wrote organ masterpieces, including Johann Sebastian Bach of Germany. During this period, organists played along with singers in operas and other musical performances. Large organs were played in churches, while small organs were popular at home and at public events.

By the early 1800's, small organs had lost their popularity. Many composers preferred the **piano** or an orchestra to create a larger variety of sounds. However, the organ's popularity was revived in the early 1900's with the help of Albert Schweitzer, an accomplished German organist who gave popular concerts in many European cities.

In 1934, the American inventor Laurens Hammond **patented** one of the first **electronic** organs, which use electric power to create sound. Today, the electronic organ is one of the most widely played instruments in the United States. Modern pipe organs can have up to 5,000 pipes, and are considered the most powerful of all musical instruments.

Johann Sebastian Bach

Johann Sebastian Bach (1685-1750) was a famous German composer. Bach wrote hundreds of compositions, including nearly 300 religious and nonreligious choral works called *cantatas*. As a child, Bach had learned to play the clavichord and **harpsichord**. In 1703, Bach became an organist. He worked for many years as a musician for royal courts but also spent time composing his own music. About 1740, Bach developed serious eye trouble, and in his last years he was nearly blind. He died of a stroke on July 28, 1750.

Playing Music: The Keyboard

▶ The Hammered Dulcimer

A hammered dulcimer resembles the inside of a piano. Instead of using a keyboard to control the hammers, a dulcimer player strikes the strings by hand.

Many musical instruments have evolved slowly over time, making it difficult to trace where they were first invented. However, if we look at modern instruments, such as the **piano,** we can see their beginnings in much earlier instruments, such as the **hammered dulcimer** *(DUHL suh muhr).*

The hammered dulcimer is an instrument that probably originated in the Middle East during the A.D. 1100's or earlier. Though the hammered dulcimer does not use keys to produce sound, it is considered an ancestor to several modern keyboard instruments.

The hammered dulcimer has a **soundboard** with anywhere from 42 to 72 strings stretched across it. To play a dulcimer, the musician strikes the strings with wooden **hammers.** Each pair of strings sounds two different notes.

People from Turkey brought the hammered dulcimer to Europe in the 1400's, and its use became widespread throughout the continent. The dulcimer's portability and simplicity made it a popular instrument. Its design influenced the development of several important keyboard instruments, including the piano. The piano also uses hammers to strike its strings, but they are hidden inside the piano body and controlled by the keyboard.

The hammered dulcimer became popular in Europe during the **Renais-**

sance *(REHN uh sons)* between the early 1300's and late 1500's. The Renaissance was a period of great advancement in educational and artistic ideas. During this time, music blossomed into its own art form.

European **immigrants** brought the hammered dulcimer to the United States in the 1800's. Its popularity declined after World War II (1939-1945). Then in the 1960's, American folk singers began using the instrument. Today, the hammered dulcimer is played in many parts of the world.

This French painting from 1500 shows several musical instruments. The woman seated is playing a hammered dulcimer.

The mountain dulcimer became popular in the early 1800's. The strings on this type of dulcimer are plucked instead of hammered.

F U N
F A C T
The word *dulcimer* comes from the Latin and Greek words *dulce* and *melos*. Together they mean "sweet tune." American nicknames for the dulcimer include "whamadiddle," "chopping board," and "lumberjack's piano."

Playing Music: The Keyboard

▶ The Harpsichord

This harpsichord was made by Flemish artist Jan Ruckers in 1634. His family is famous for making harpsichords with a second manual, or keyboard.

Between the 1300's and 1500's, a cultural movement swept across Europe that revived art and learning in many countries. Historians now call this period the **Renaissance,** or "rebirth." During the Renaissance, live musical performances were a popular form of entertainment. A keyboard instrument called the **harpsichord** became the centerpiece of these performances.

A harpsichord looks like a small **piano,** though it can sometimes have two keyboards, called manuals. Both the piano and the harpsichord produce sound when their metal strings are caused to vibrate. However, the two instruments create sound differently. The piano produces sound when its **hammers** strike or push against its strings. The harpsichord creates sound when its strings are plucked by a small piece of quill or leather.

Because of their differences in size and the way in which they create sound, the piano and harpsichord have very different tones. The smaller harpsichord creates a clearer, livelier tone than the piano.

No one knows exactly who invented the harpsichord. The instrument dates back to the 1300's. During the 1400's, Flanders, a region in Belgium and France, became famous for building harpsichords. Later, Italian craftsmen built harpsichords. Eventually, the art of harpsichord-

Many musicians composed music for the harpsichord during the height of its popularity.

making spread throughout France, Germany, and England.

The design of harpsichords has changed over time. By the 1600's, most harpsichords had two manuals (keyboards), and they also had three strings for each note.

Harpsichords with a greater range of tones were developed in the 1700's. During this time, the harpsichord became one of the most important musical instruments in Europe. It was often used to accompany dramatic performances, such as operas.

During the height of the harpsichord's popularity, such famous composers as Johann Sebastian Bach (*bahk*), George Frideric Handel, and Joseph Haydn (*HYD uhn*) wrote many pieces for the harpsichord.

By the late 1700's, the harpsichord was being steadily replaced by the piano. Before long, harpsichord music had all but died out. However, the harpsichord became popular again after the 1940's and has regained some of its musical importance today.

 **A CLOSER LOOK**

Another popular keyboard instrument during the Renaissance was the clavichord (*KLAV uh kawrd*). The clavichord produces sound with metal blades that strike the instrument's wire strings when its keys are pressed down. The instrument produces soft tones, so it was used for musical practices and entertaining small gatherings rather than public concerts.

Playing Music: The Keyboard

▶ The Piano

This grand piano was made in Salzburg, Austria, in 1788. Austria has long been a center for the musical arts.

During the late 1700's, the **harpsichord** and **organ** were used less frequently in musical performances. This was largely due to the invention of a new keyboard instrument that was the direct forerunner of the modern **piano.**

The piano has its roots in earlier keyboard instruments. Like the dulcimer and the harpsichord, a piano produces sound by causing metal strings to vibrate. However, the strings of a piano are struck by little **hammers** instead of being plucked by a piece of quill or leather, like those of a harpsichord. These hammers can return to their resting positions quickly, allowing the piano player to quickly repeat a note. And because the loudness of a tone depends on how hard the musician strikes the keys, the player can also make the note soft or loud.

In 1709, an Italian instrument maker named Bartolomeo Cristofori invented the *gravicembalo col piano e forte*, which means "harpsichord with soft and loud." Over time, the name was shortened to *pianoforte*. Cristofori's instrument was the ancestor of the modern piano.

Between the late 1700's and early 1800's, musical instrument makers improved Cristofori's pianoforte. Some improvements created louder and richer tones than the pianoforte. Others improved the action of the piano's hammers. The American inventor Alpheus Babcock made a large cast-iron frame piano in 1825. He also developed a method of cross-stringing pianos. In 1855, a German-born piano maker named Henry E. Steinway combined all of these inventions into one piano.

The piano has been called "the king of the musical instruments" because it can produce a greater range of musical sounds than most other instruments. It can produce the lowest tone of the double bassoon and the highest note of the piccolo. And next to the pipe organ, the piano is the largest instrument.

Because the piano offered a much larger range of sounds than other keyboard instruments, composers quickly abandoned the harpsichord to write music for the piano. Soon piano playing became a major form of entertainment in public performances and in people's homes. Today, the piano is used in classical music, jazz, rock, and other kinds of music.

Piano concerts and recitals are still popular forms of entertainment all over the world.

A CLOSER LOOK

In the late 1800's, inventors developed a type of piano that could play itself! Player pianos are operated by a roll of paper that has patterns of holes that correspond to different notes. The paper moves over a cylinder that also has holes. A stream of pressurized air is sucked through the matching holes in the roll and cylinder. This causes the piano's hammers to strike the different strings to create music. The performances of many great pianists in the late 1800's and early 1900's were captured on player rolls.

Playing Music: The Keyboard

▶ Electronic Keyboards

American blues musician Sunnyland Slim sits at the keyboard of his Wurlitzer electric piano in the 1970's.

In the early 1900's, advances in technology led to several new types of keyboard instruments. Some of these instruments used electric power to **amplify** their sound, and others used electric power to create their sound.

In the 1930's, an American named Benjamin Miessner created one of the first **electric pianos.** This instrument can be played just like a regular **piano,** but its sound is turned into **electronic** signals and then amplified through speakers.

Miessner created his electric piano by placing **electromagnetic** devices on each string inside a piano. He also added reeds (hollow tubes) into which the pianist could blow air to create a more powerful tone.

Many piano manufacturers in the United States saw the importance of Miessner's creation. The Rudolph Wurlitzer Company bought the technology and used it to develop its own electric piano, called the Wurlitzer.

The Wurlitzer included felt **hammers** that stroked the metal reeds inside the piano, causing them to vibrate. These vibrations were picked up and converted into electric energy and then carried to speakers that were built into the piano. Wurlitzer's first electric piano was released in the 1950's.

During World War II (1939-1945), an American music teacher named Harold Rhodes developed an electric piano for wounded soldiers. Rhodes designed the piano so that soldiers could play it in bed as a form of therapy. In about 1956, Rhodes developed an improved electric piano, which he later sold **commercially.**

The design of the electric piano continued to improve throughout the 1900's. Soon, electric pianos became a popular way of playing music. Pop and rock bands in the 1960's and 1970's liked the distinctive, clear sound of the Wurlitzer. Many famous jazz musicians of the 1970's preferred the Rhodes.

In the 1980's, the **synthesizer** expanded the capabilities of keyboard instruments even further. Unlike the electric piano, the synthesizer creates its sound through electric signals that are then amplified. With a synthesizer, musicians could produce a wide variety of sounds. Each key on a synthesizer is capable of playing more than one note at time.

Today, people can also play **digital** pianos, which are made to sound like traditional pianos but can have the capabilities of electronic instruments, such as synthesizers. Digital pianos are smaller and lighter than traditional pianos and do not need tuning.

Synthesizers are a big part of modern music. They can make a wide variety of sounds and are often used in place of other instruments.

Most digital pianos are smaller and less expensive than traditional pianos.

Capturing Music

▶ The Microphone

The microphone was an essential part of Alexander Graham Bell's new invention, the telephone.

People have been playing music for thousands of years, but it was not until the 1900's that they were able to record music. The first invention that would lead to recorded music was the microphone.

A microphone is a device that changes sound into electric energy. This energy travels over wires or through the air until it reaches a loudspeaker. The speaker then changes the electric energy back into sound.

The invention of the microphone coincided with the invention of the telephone. A Scottish-born inventor named Alexander Graham Bell is credited with the invention of the telephone. Its development largely grew out of experiments Bell conducted in the 1870's with a communication tool called the **telegraph.**

The telegraph was an instrument developed in the 1800's that could send coded messages over wires using electric energy. Bell had been working to create a device that could send several telegraph messages over one wire. By accident, Bell discovered that he could send his voice over the wire through electric energy. This discovery led to the invention of the telephone—and with it, the first microphone.

Many scientists worked to improve the microphone by using different substances to create an **electric current.** Today, there are many different types of microphones. Some pick up sound from all directions, while others are sensitive to sound from only certain directions. There are even microphones that can be used to listen to sounds transmitted underwater.

Microphones are used in all telephones, in public-address systems, and in **broadcast** radio and television shows. They are also used in recording the sound for **motion pictures** and in making **compact discs (CD's)** and tape recordings.

The microphone became the symbol of radio in its early days.

When **sound waves** enter a microphone, a metal sheet called a diaphragm is caused to vibrate. These vibrations cause changes to the electric current flowing to the speakers or recording equipment. The sound can then be recorded, reproduced, or **amplified**.

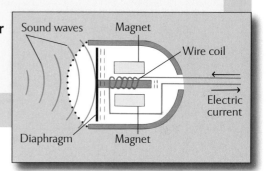

Sound waves
Magnet
Wire coil
Electric current
Diaphragm
Magnet

Microphones can capture sounds up close or far away. Some microphones have fuzzy protective covers to reduce wind and background noise.

Capturing Music

▶ The Phonograph

Up until the late 1800's, music could only be heard as live entertainment. This changed with the invention of the **phonograph,** a machine that can reproduce recorded sound.

In 1877, the American inventor Thomas Edison developed the first practical phonograph, which could record and play back sound. Edison's device recorded sound on tinfoil wrapped around a metal cylinder, which the operator rotated with a hand crank. The device also had a needle attached to a vibrating disc, which was placed against the rotating cylinder.

This French advertisement from 1905 shows the phonograph's quick evolution.

Thomas Edison sits with his new invention, the phonograph, in 1878.

When a person spoke into a mouthpiece, the **sound waves** from the person's voice would cause the needle to vibrate. This movement made dents in the tinfoil on the cylinder, which recorded the sound.

A similar setup was used to play back the sound. Another needle attached to a disc was placed against the rotating cylinder. The dents in the tinfoil made the needle and the disc vibrate and play back the original sounds.

In 1887, a German-born inventor named Emile Berliner improved Edison's design. He developed the first successful phonograph, which used disc-shaped records that stored the likeness of the original sound waves as jagged waves on its surface.

To play a record, the phonograph rotates the disc while a needle rides in the small grooves on the record. The waves in the groove make the needle vibrate. Speakers change these vibrations back into sound.

The next improvement to phonographs came in 1925, with the introduction of electrically recorded records. Manufacturers also started making phonographs with electric motors and **amplifiers.**

The invention of the phonograph and records led to the development of the music recording **industry.** Eventually, the recording industry produced records of musicians from around the world. This inspired many musicians to create new musical sounds and styles of playing.

Records were a popular form of entertainment until the 1980's, when **compact discs (CD's)** were introduced. CD's quickly became popular, causing the sale and production of phonographs and records to fall sharply. Still, many music lovers today prefer the warmer, richer sounds of records to other forms of musical recording.

Portable record players, like this one from 1963, folded up like a suitcase.

Capturing Music

▶ The Tape Recorder

English school-boys listen to a tape recording in 1964.

In the late 1800's and early 1900's, people continued to look for new and improved ways to record sound. These improvements led to the development of the **tape recorder,** a device that can record sound on magnetic tape.

In 1898, an **engineer** from Denmark named Valdemar Poulsen invented the first machine for recording sound. Poulsen's machine used an **electromagnet** to make a sound recording on steel wire.

Despite Poulsen's success, his invention did not become widely used for more than 30 years. This was mainly due to the popularity of the **phonograph.** However, Poulsen's work was an important step in the development of the tape recorder.

In the early 1900's, many scientists worked to improve the magnetic tape recorder. By the early 1930's, a small number of sound recorders were produced **commercially.** However, these first recorders used steel wire and steel ribbon, materials that are difficult to handle and store.

In 1935, German engineers introduced a new magnetic recording machine that used plastic magnetic tape. One side of the plastic tape had tiny magnetic units that formed patterns during the recording process. These patterns produced electric signals that sounded like the original sounds when played back.

By 1950, the radio and recording **industries** were making widespread use of tape recorders. Manufacturers began to produce tape recorders for home use in the mid-1950's. Ten years later, the development of small **cassette** tapes revolutionized the recording industry. During the 1980's, portable cassette players made cassette tapes popular for everyday use.

Today, tape recorders can record and play back sound, pictures, video, and other kinds of data. Tape recorders are still used by the music recording industry and radio and television **broadcasts.** They are also used to record information from scientific equipment and computers.

By the late 1980's, the invention of the **compact disc (CD)** led to a drop in popularity of cassette tapes. In the late 1990's, **digital** music recordings, which can be played on computers and digital music players, all but replaced the use of cassette tapes for personal use. (See The Compact Disc, pages 22-23.)

Personal cassette players became popular in the 1980's.

A CLOSER LOOK

Recording tape consists of a plastic base coated with metallic particles that are easily magnetized. In recording, electric signals from a microphone create a magnetic field around a gap in the recording head. The field magnetizes the particles on the tape into a pattern like that of the sound waves entering the microphone.

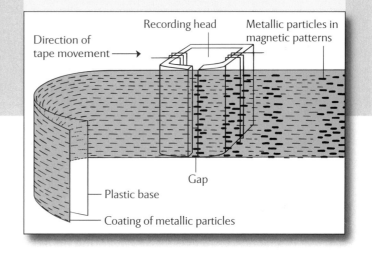

Direction of tape movement

Recording head

Metallic particles in magnetic patterns

Gap

Plastic base

Coating of metallic particles

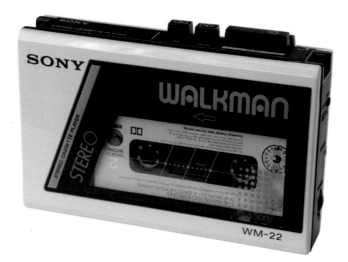

Capturing Music

▶ The Compact Disc

Compact discs brought digital music to the radio and to people's homes. CD's are smaller and can hold more information than records.

I n the early 1980's, the invention of the **compact disc (CD)** changed the way people listen to music once again. A compact disc is a round, flat disc on which recorded music or other information is stored in the form of a **digital** (numerical) code.

In the 1960's, the American scientist James T. Russell worked to find a better way to listen to music. A music fan, Russell was frustrated with the sound quality and fragile nature of his **phonograph** records. Russell knew that playing a record caused some wear and tear to it. To play sound from a record, a needle called a stylus must come into contact with it. This can cause the record to become scratched.

Russell wanted to design a system where a record could be played without a needle. He knew that he could use a powerful beam of light instead of the stylus to reproduce sound. He also knew that he could record the information digitally (using a number code). Information that is stored digitally takes up very little space.

In 1970, Russell **patented** the first compact disc. Eventually, he sold this technology to several companies. The **electronics** companies Sony and Philips introduced the compact disc to Japan and Germany in 1982. The following year, the CD spread to other countries in Europe and the United States.

By the mid 1990's, CD's had largely replaced phonograph records and **cassette** tapes. The development of portable CD players and CD players in cars increased their use.

Today, many people listen to music on devices called **portable media players,** which store music as digital files. These players are often battery-powered and small enough to fit in a shirt pocket. People can store and listen to digital music files on a computer. They can download albums and individual tracks using the **Internet.**

Today, people can save music onto portable media players and arrange songs any way they like.

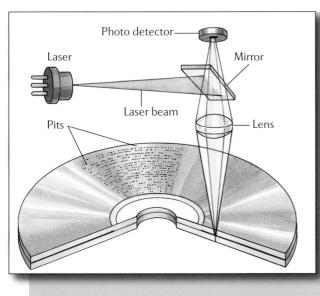

Photo detector — Laser — Mirror — Laser beam — Lens — Pits

A CLOSER LOOK

A compact disc has stored information in the form of a digital code. The CD player reads this information with a **laser** (a very powerful beam of light). A separate device translates the reflected light into an electric signal, which is used to produce sound.

Painting

▶ Tempera Paint

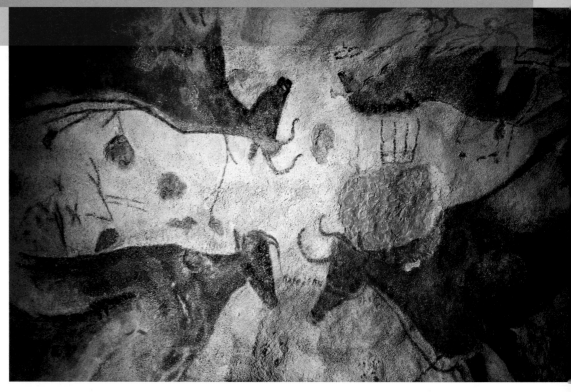

Some of the best examples of pre-historic cave paintings were discovered in France in 1940.

Along with music, painting is one of the oldest art forms in human history. The oldest known paintings date back 30,000 years. Most of these paintings show hunting scenes with large animals, such as horses, buffalo, and deer.

Since prehistoric times, people have arranged colors on surfaces in ways that express their ideas. The painting process today is not much different from what it was thousands of years ago. To make paint, a powdered color called a **pigment** is mixed with another substance. The paint is then thinned using a **solvent,** such as turpentine. It is then applied using brushes or other tools to a surface.

One of the oldest types of paint is called tempera (*TEHM puhr uh*). The ancient Egyptians, ancient Greeks, and ancient **Romans** all used tempera paint. To make tempera paint, an artist mixes water with dried pigments to make a paste. The artist then adds fresh egg to the paste. Like egg yolk, tempera dries almost immediately.

Since most surfaces absorb the paint very quickly, the artist must first cover the painting surface with one or

In this detail of an Italian painting from the 1300's, tempera paint gives the impression that the figure is glowing.

more coats of a special paintlike material called a ground. A common ground for use with tempera is a mixture of white chalk and glue.

Images painted with tempera are sharp and exact. When the tempera dries, it combines with the chalk and glue mixture, creating a surface that seems to glow.

Artists during the **Renaissance** (A.D. 1300's-1500's) used tempera to paint many beautiful portraits of important people. At the time, painting was the only way to record a person's likeness. Artists also used tempera to create paintings of religious figures, such as the Virgin Mary.

Tempera painting was largely replaced in the 1500's by oil painting. However, it is still used to paint religious pictures. Several modern artists, including Ben Shahn and Andrew Wyeth, have used tempera to take advantage of its soft, warm tones.

Some modern tempera paints are a mixture of pigments, water, and chalk.

Painting

▶ Oil Paint

An artist uses her palette knife to mix oil paints.

Oil paints are made by mixing powdered **pigments** with a vegetable oil, such as linseed oil. No one knows exactly where oil paints developed. In 2008, scientists discovered the oldest known oil painting in an area of Afghanistan. **Archaeologists** believe the painting was made around A.D. 650.

In Northern Europe, oil painting dates back to at least to the 1100's. In the 1500's, artists began to make oil painting their main medium (way of painting). The popularity of oil paints quickly spread throughout Europe, replacing tempera painting almost completely.

Many color shades were impossible before the development of oil painting techniques. And unlike tempera, oil paint can be easily blended onto a painting surface to create a smooth transition between light and dark, or between different colors. Oil paint also dries more slowly than tempera. This allows artists to work almost endlessly to perfect the image.

Artists often start an oil painting by laying down a thin layer of paint on a surface. This serves as the base for the other layers of paint and helps define color. The famous Italian painter Leonardo da Vinci used a base of gray-green tones under his famous portrait, the *Mona Lisa*.

Some artists use a special painting technique where they apply the oil paint very thickly. Because of its thickness, the paint becomes three-dimensional. It also keeps the texture of the brush or stroke from the **palette knife.**

Jan van Eyck's oil paintings, such as *The Portrait of Giovanni Arnolfini and his Wife Giovanna Genami* (1434), were famous for their realistic detail.

Early on, European oil painters concentrated on painting the human figure in heroic and religious scenes, working hard to create paintings with careful detail. During the **Renaissance,** artists studied the human body to help them create lifelike human figures on canvas.

Toward the end of the 1800's, a new art movement started in Europe called **Impressionism.** Impressionist artists preferred to paint everyday scenes, often working outdoors. They did not blend color like the old master artists. Instead, they used short brush strokes of pure color. This created an effect of strong color vibration. Impressionists emphasized dramatic overall effects rather than details. Their paintings often appear to glow with light.

Oil paints were used throughout the 1800's. Artists would have to wait until the early 1900's for the invention of a type of paint that gave artists even more options for painting styles.

Vincent van Gogh was a master of texture and color, as seen here in *The Starry Night,* painted in 1889.

Painting

▶ Acrylic Paint

Acrylic paints are safer and easier to use than other types of paints. They can resemble oil paint or water colors, and they wash out with soap and water.

Acrylic *(uh KRIHL ihk)* paints are one of the most recent advances in paint materials. They quickly became popular after their development in the 1950's.

In the early 1900's, two Mexican artists named Diego Rivera and José Clemente Orozco *(hoh SAY klay MAYN tay oh ROHS koh)* were using a painting technique called **fresco.** Fresco was first used by artists during the **Renaissance.** The paintings, which were called frescoes, were painted on a damp surface of **plaster.** One of the most famous examples of fresco was painted by the Italian artist Michelangelo on the ceiling of the Sistine Chapel in the early 1500's.

In the 1920's, Rivera, Orozco, and other Mexican artists used fresco techniques to paint **murals** (pictures on walls or ceilings). However, the sun, rain, and humid air in Mexico caused the paint to crack and peel.

Frustrated with the limitations of their painting materials, Mexican muralists (mural painters) began to experiment with paints that were made of different substances. In 1936, a Mexican artist named David Siqueiros *(see KAY raws)* organized a workshop in New York City to experiment with **synthetic** (human-made) paints.

By the mid-1950's, researchers in the United States had developed a way to mix a type of plastic called acrylic resin with a **solvent** to create acrylic paint. These new acrylic paints had many advantages. Unlike oil paint, there is no chemical reaction between acrylic paint and a painting surface, so artists do not have to prime (prepare) it before painting.

Acrylic paint can be used on almost any surface. It is extremely tough and dries rapidly. And once it is dry, acrylic paint is completely resistant to water. Acrylics can also be used for many styles of painting. For example, an artist can use acrylics to create paintings that look almost identical to oil paintings. The artist can also thin acrylic paints with water to create paintings that resemble water colors.

Because acrylic paints are water-based, they are far less harmful than oil paints. Artists can use soap and water to clean their brushes instead of a solvent, which is necessary to remove oil paint from a brush.

Today, people can choose from tempera, oil, and acrylic paints to fit any style in which they wish to paint. Though the materials used for painting have not greatly changed, they have been used in countless new ways to create unique masterpieces.

Diego Rivera, shown here in 1943, was famous for his murals that portrayed Mexican life and history.

In 1988, Portuguese artist Paula Rego used acrylic paint to capture light and darkness in *The Dance.*

Capturing Images

▶ The Camera Obscura

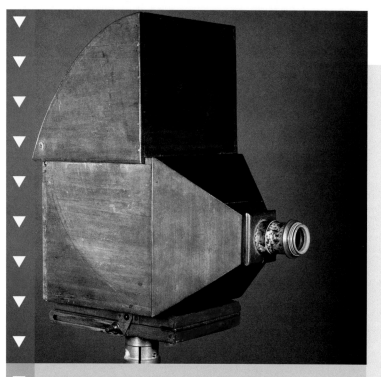

This camera obscura is simply a lightproof box with a lens and a mirror inside.

Since prehistoric times, people have depicted the world around them through art. At first, they drew paintings on cave walls. Later, they developed new painting and drawing techniques.

Though the art of painting and drawing dates back many thousands of years, the art of capturing images through **photography** and **motion pictures** is relatively new. However, its beginnings date back more than 2,000 years. One of the first important inventions in capturing images was the **camera obscura** (*ob SKYUR uh*), a small chamber or box that could reproduce the image of an object using light.

In the 400's B.C., a Chinese philosopher named Mo Di made an important discovery. He saw that when light was reflected from an object and passed through a pinhole (tiny hole), an upside-down image of the object would appear on a nearby surface.

Around 330 B.C., the Greek philosopher Aristotle noticed the same thing during a solar eclipse, which occurs when the sun appears to become dark as the moon passes between the sun and Earth. As Aristotle sat under a tree during the eclipse, he noticed several images of the sun on the ground. The movement of the leaves over his head created small openings, which acted like pinholes for the sun's rays.

The camera obscura was the forerunner to the camera. Like the camera, the camera obscura was a lightproof box with an aperture (opening) at one end. Light reflected from an object enters the camera obscura through the lens, which focuses the light rays into an image on the inside of the box. Light rays from the top of the object make up the lower part of the image, and those from the bottom form the upper part. Because of this, the image is upside down.

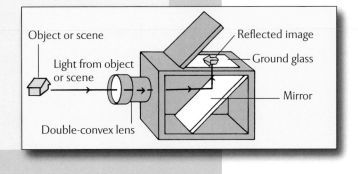

After making this discovery, Aristotle experimented with letting the sun enter a square opening against a dark background. He found that the image of the sun remained round. His description of this experiment paved the way to the camera obscura.

Eventually, inventors created small boxes that could **project** images. In the 1500's, the addition of a mirror and a lens to the camera obscura flipped the image so that it would be right-side up. An adjustable opening controlled the size of the pinhole.

Unfortunately, a camera obscura could only project images. But over the next 300 years, people worked to develop methods that could make these images permanent.

In this illustration from 1887, children view an outdoor scene through a camera obscura.

Capturing Images

▶ The Camera

Daguerreotype was the first practical, popular method of photography. Daguerreotype portraits were tremendously popular during the 1840's and 1850's.

In 1717, a German scientist named Johann Schulze made an important discovery. He noticed that silver salts turned dark when exposed to light. About 50 years later, a scientist from Sweden named Carl Scheele showed that the changes caused in the salts by light could be made permanent by chemical treatment. These discoveries would lead to the development of **photography.**

In 1826, a French inventor named Joseph Niépce (*Nyehps*) created a method for capturing permanent images inside a **camera obscura.** He took a metal plate and coated it with a light-sensitive chemical substance. This served as the **film** onto which he could capture an image. Niépce then placed the plate in the camera. Eight hours later, the view from his window appeared on the film, creating the world's oldest surviving photograph.

A French artist named Louis Daguerre (*dah GAIR*) improved Niépce's process. In the 1830's, he placed a sheet of silver-coated copper inside a camera obscura. Then he removed the film and developed the image with the fumes of heated mercury (a liquid metal). In the final step, he treated the image with table salt to prevent fading.

Daguerre's images were called **daguerreotypes** (*duh GEHR uh typs*). At first, these pictures needed 5 to 40 minutes of **exposure** inside the camera. Later, the process was improved, and the time was cut to less than a minute.

In 1839, a British inventor named William Henry Fox Talbot announced his development of light-sensitive paper. The paper produced a **negative** image, which showed the lights and darks reversed. A positive image could then be made from the negative image.

A friend of Fox Talbot's named his invention *photography*. In Greek, *photography* means to "write or draw with light." Fox Talbot's friend also suggested using a chemical to make the image permanent. Daguerre and Fox Talbot took his advice and used the chemical to **fix** their images.

Daguerre's methods produced better images than Fox Talbot's paper prints. However, Fox Talbot's method of negative-to-positive images became the foundation of modern photography. Its advantage was that numerous paper prints could be made from one exposure. These prints could be pasted into books and other types of printed materials.

In recent years, camera technology has improved in many ways. New lens designs and improved methods to fix images have simplified photography. The invention of **digital** cameras in the mid-1900's would simplify these methods even further. (See pages 42-43.)

William Henry Fox Talbot (far right) readies his camera.

Mathew Brady

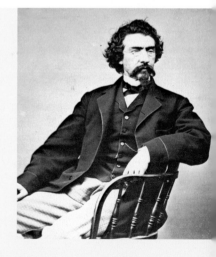

Mathew B. Brady (1823?-1896) was a famous American photographer. Brady is known for taking photographs of historical events and people. He opened a photography studio in 1844 in New York City.

By 1851, Brady's eyesight had grown too poor for him to operate a camera, so he hired photographers to help him. During the Civil War, Brady hired up to 100 photographers. They took thousands of pictures of battlefield scenes and camp life. Brady is also famous for photographs taken of American presidents.

Capturing Images

▶ Film Development

Until 1871, photographers had to take the darkroom with them.

In the mid-1800's, a British photographer named Frederick S. Archer set out to improve the process of making photographs. He wanted to keep the sharpness of images produced by a **daguerreotype,** but he also wanted to be able to reproduce these images.

Archer coated a glass plate with substances that made the plate light sensitive. He then placed the plate inside the camera, exposed it to light, and developed the image while the plate was still wet. The result was a sharp, long-lasting glass **negative** that could be used to easily reproduce an image. This technique became known as the **wet-plate process.**

Photographers who used the wet-plate process had to develop their images immediately after **exposure.** Because of this, they needed a darkroom so that the plate would stay wet during exposure and developing. Some photographers took their darkrooms with them in wagons when they traveled.

In 1871, a British doctor named Richard L. Maddox created a new process for developing photographs. He used an **emulsion** of gelatin, which dried on the photographic plate before it was exposed. This process came to be known as the **dry-plate process.**

The dry-plate process allowed photographers to wait before developing photographs, so they no longer had to travel with their darkrooms. Gelatin also reduced exposure time.

The dry-plate process changed camera design. Before its invention, the negative and the printed photo-

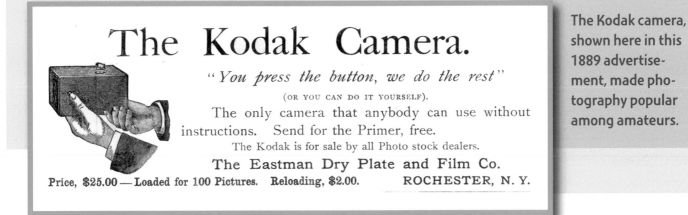

The Kodak Camera.

"You press the button, we do the rest"

(OR YOU CAN DO IT YOURSELF).

The only camera that anybody can use without instructions.   Send for the Primer, free.

The Kodak is for sale by all Photo stock dealers.

The Eastman Dry Plate and Film Co.

Price, $25.00 — Loaded for 100 Pictures.   Reloading, $2.00.   ROCHESTER, N. Y.

The Kodak camera, shown here in this 1889 advertisement, made photography popular among amateurs.

graph had to be the same size. Now photographers could enlarge the image by **projecting** it from the **negative** onto paper coated with gelatin. This meant that negatives could be smaller, which led to smaller cameras.

In late 1800's, an American inventor named George Eastman invented the first roll of **film.** Unlike the dry plate, the roll of film was flexible and lightweight. While the dry plate could record only one image, Eastman's roll of film could record 100 images.

In 1888, Eastman introduced the Kodak box camera, which included the new roll of film. When the film was used up, the photographer would simply send the camera to a processing plant for development. The prints were then sent back to the owner, along with a freshly loaded camera.

The Kodak camera became an instant success. It eliminated the need for people to process their own photographs, making it possible for anyone to take pictures.

Advances in cameras and film materials would eventually lead to an important new art form called **motion pictures.**

George Eastman

George Eastman (1854-1932) was an American businessman and inventor. In 1860, Eastman moved to Rochester, New York. There, he developed a dry photographic plate, which he began manufacturing in 1880. In 1888, Eastman introduced the Kodak camera, which used a flexible roll of gelatin film. By the early 1900's, the Eastman Kodak Company had become the largest photographic film and camera producer in the world.

Capturing Images

▶ Motion Pictures

In 1878, Eadweard Muybridge used a row of cameras to capture the motion of a running horse.

After the development of **photography** in the 1800's, inventors were inspired to develop technology that could produce moving images on **film.** Soon, **motion pictures** would be born.

With a motion picture, a series of images appear to move when played through a film **projector** or video player. These images were originally recorded on a type of **film** called celluloid.

Eadweard Muybridge (*EHD wurd MY brihj*) was a British photographer who worked in California in the late 1800's. Muybridge created the first successful photographs of motion in 1877 and 1878.

Muybridge took a series of photographs of a running horse by setting up a row of cameras and attaching strings to each shutter, a device that opens and closes in front of the film in a camera. The shutter is used to change the length of an **exposure.** When the horse ran past the cameras, it broke each string and tripped the shutter.

Muybridge's accomplishment inspired inventors in several countries to work toward developing devices for recording and playing movie images. Their efforts led to the invention of a variety of motion-picture cameras and projectors by the mid-1890's.

In 1893, the American inventor Thomas Edison and his company made the first **commercial** motion-picture machine. Edison called his machine the kinetoscope (*kih NEHT uh skohp*). The kinetoscope was basically a cabinet with a tiny hole, which the viewer could look through to watch a series of black-and-white films.

Kinetoscope parlors opened in several cities. However, new projection machines that showed greatly enlarged pictures on a screen soon replaced

The kinetoscope was a dazzling novelty. The big hit of 1894 was a five-second-long movie of a man sneezing!

them. These parlors allowed large crowds to watch a film at the same time.

Seeing films became a popular pastime. Film **projectionists** traveled to bring motion pictures to smaller cities and towns, where they showed dramatized folktales and re-creations of current news events.

The first films did not have recorded sound. Often, someone played the **piano** or spoke. Other times, actors spoke the lines during a show. Later, movies had printed lines of dialogue, or descriptions of action. These were easily translated into other languages so that the films could be shown worldwide.

Modern motion pictures serve many purposes. People enjoy making their own movies and recording important events with small motion-picture cameras called **camcorders.** Documentaries present educational information in a dramatic and entertaining way. Television stations and cable TV networks use motion pictures to inform and entertain viewers. Today, motion pictures are a huge **industry.**

A CLOSER LOOK

Inventors around the world worked to create a device to capture and show motion pictures. They included Thomas Armat, Thomas Edison, C. Francis Jenkins, and Woodville Latham in the United States; William Friese-Greene and Robert W. Paul in the United Kingdom; and Etienne-Jules Marey and the brothers Louis Jean and Auguste Lumière in France. On December 28, 1895, the Lumière brothers showed a projected motion picture in a Paris café. Thomas Edison, adapting Armat's projector, showed the first projected motion picture in the United States in a New York City music hall on April 23, 1896.

Capturing Images

▶ Animation

In the early 1800's, inventors around the world created several early animation devices, including the phenakistoscope (top) and praxioscope (bottom).

With the growing popularity of **motion pictures,** filmmakers and artists began to look for new techniques to create motion on **film.** One technique, called **animation,** became an art form of its own. It allowed filmmakers to show things that could not be shown in live action.

Long before the first motion pictures of the late 1800's, a scientist in Belgium named Joseph Antoine Plateau invented the first example of animation. In 1832, he created a toy called the phenakistoscope (*FEHN uh KIHS tuh skohp*), which was basically a notched wheel attached to a handle. One side of the wheel had a series of drawings. When the wheel was held in front of a mirror and spun, the mirrored images appeared to move. The phenakistoscope and similar devices were forerunners to animated film.

In the early days of animated movies, a filmmaker would photograph a series of drawings or objects one by one. The position of the object was changed slightly for each new **frame** of film. When the filmstrip was shown through a **projector,** the pictures appeared to move.

In 1914, an American animator named John Randolph Bray began to change the process of creating animation. Under his direction, studios hired large staffs, and the animation process was treated like an **assembly line,** with each animator responsible for a certain part.

Bray worked with an animator named Earl Hurd, who had developed an animation technique that separated the figures from the background. This way, backgrounds could be used over and over again. Animators only had to redraw the figures, saving much time and money.

As animation improved, American movie studios began creating cartoon characters that appeared regularly in animated films. But due to the popularity of television during the mid 1950's, interest in animated feature-length films declined through the 1960's.

Animated feature films regained popularity between the 1970's and 1990's with films like *Who Framed Roger Rabbit, The Little Mermaid, Beauty and the Beast,* and *The Lion King.* Today, animated films are some of the biggest hits in movie theaters.

Walt Disney

Walt Disney (1901–1966) was one of the most famous producers of animated films. He created such famous cartoon characters as Mickey Mouse, Minnie Mouse, Donald Duck, Goofy, and Pluto.

Disney founded his cartoon studio in 1923. In 1928, he produced the first animated cartoon with a **sound track.** Disney's studio created some of the most famous animated feature films, including *Dumbo, Bambi,* and *Cinderella.* His 1937 animated film, *Snow White and the Seven Dwarfs,* became one of the most popular films in movie history.

Since the 1980's, computer animation has created exciting new animated films. Animators can create films entirely on a computer, combined with traditional types of animation, or combined with live action.

Modern-day computer animation can be almost lifelike.

Capturing Images

▶ Sound Tracks

Inventor Charles A. Hoxie shows a child movie star how to record his voice on the "talking machine" in 1923.

As **motion pictures** became more and more popular, moviemakers looked for new ways to improve their **films.** One way to do so was to add a **sound track.** Early films were silent and often accompanied by music or spoken dialogue. However, silent films would soon become a thing of the past.

In the early 1900's, **engineers** in the United States and Germany worked to develop a way to add recorded sound to movies. By the mid-1920's, motion pictures with recorded sound started to appear in theaters.

The Jazz Singer (1927) was the first film with sound to get everyone's attention. Even though only a few scenes had sound, people were amazed to hear Al Jolson, a popular entertainer, sing and talk. The sound for the movie was recorded on a disc and mechanically synchronized (made to go at the same rate) with the film.

The early system of recorded sound was soon replaced by one that used **electronic** signals. These signals were used to record the sound directly onto the filmstrip. By 1929, use of the sound-on-film system was widespread.

With the addition of sound, filmmakers had to change their methods of making movies. Cameras had to be enclosed in a soundproof box so they would not pick up background noise.

Piano players helped create the mood and atmosphere for silent pictures.

The far left of this strip of film (at right) shows the sound recording for the movie.

Film directors also needed to learn to use sound effectively. People in the motion picture **industry** quickly made these adjustments.

Sound technology changed **Holly-wood.** Now films needed dialogue writers, actors with voice training, and speech coaches. A number of silent movie stars had trouble with the transition. They discovered they were not wanted because they had strong accents or their voices did not match their looks.

In 1940, Disney's animated film *Fantasia* was the first motion picture to use surround sound, a standard feature in theaters today. Surround-sound speakers encircle the audience. Prior to the development of surround sound, speakers were only at the front of the theater. With this new sound system, viewers had sound coming at them from every direction.

Today, sound quality is an important part of motion pictures.

Capturing Images

▶ Digital Cameras

With digital photography, people can check the image immediately after taking a picture.

By the end of the 1900's, scientists had developed **digital** cameras for **photography** and **motion pictures.** A digital camera stores images digitally (in numeric code) rather than on **film.**

Scientists were using digital imaging as far back as the 1950's. In 1975, an American **engineer** named Steven Sasson invented the first digital **still camera.** Sasson worked for the Eastman Kodak Company, which had introduced its box camera and roll of film in 1888.

Digital still cameras use an **electronic** chip to store images. The images can then be downloaded and viewed on a computer or television screen and printed on paper.

The first **commercial** digital cameras were expensive and produced images that were not as high quality as film images, so they were not very popular. But as technology improved and prices dropped, sales of digital still cameras rose dramatically. Most news photographers switched to digital cameras in the mid-1990's. Commercial photographers soon followed.

By the 1990's, personal computers were common in homes. Many of them had graphics software for editing and storing digital images.

Digital **camcorders** became available for personal and professional use in the 1990's. Some filmmakers have switched to digital camcorders, though film cameras are still more commonly used.

Digital imaging is an especially exciting technology for photographers. Computer programs let them make changes to digital images in countless ways. Parts of one image can be added to another, colors can be changed, or images can be distorted.

Digital video cameras today can be nearly as small as digital still cameras.

Despite these advantages, some photographers prefer film cameras, which still have advantages over digital cameras in some respects. For example, many film cameras offer a higher dynamic range than digital cameras. Dynamic range is the ability to capture extremely bright details and extremely dark details in the same photograph.

A **CLOSER** LOOK

Digital cameras offer several advantages over film cameras. They allow the photographer to see an image immediately after taking the picture. If the photographer does not like the image, he or she can simply delete it and reshoot the picture. Digital cameras are also cheaper to run than film cameras, since the user does not have to purchase film or pay processing costs. Digital photographs can be e-mailed, posted on the **Internet,** or printed at home. In addition, a digital camera enables the photographer to edit the picture on a computer. With a film camera, each adjustment of these qualities requires a new roll or sheet of film.

Important Dates in the Arts

c. 30,000 B.C. First instances of cave paintings in Australia, France, Spain, Italy, and Portugal.

c. 10,000 B.C. People made flutes out of hollow bones.

c. 200 B.C. The Greek engineer Ctesibius designed the hydraulis.

c. 400 B.C. The Chinese philosopher Mo Di discovered the inverted image.

c. 330 B.C. The Greek philosopher Aristotle described the first camera obscura.

A.D. 1300's The harpsichord was invented.

1500's European artists adopted oil paint as their preferred medium.

1500's A mirror and lens were added to the camera obscura.

1709 The Italian musician Bartolomeo Cristofori invented the pianoforte.

1826 The French inventor Joseph Niépce made the first photograph.

1832 The Belgian scientist Joseph Antoine Plateau invented the phenakistoscope.

1830's The French artist Louis Daguerre developed the daguerreotype process.

1839 The British inventor William H. Fox Talbot developed light-sensitive paper.

1851 The British photographer Frederick S. Archer invented the wet-plate process for photographic plates.

1871 The British doctor Richard L. Maddox invented the dry-plate process for photographic plates.

1875 The Scottish-born inventor Alexander Graham Bell invented the telephone (and microphone).

1877 Thomas Edison invented the first practical phonograph.

1888 The American inventor George Eastman introduced the Kodak box camera.

1896 Thomas Edison showed the first projected motion picture in the United States.

1898 The Danish engineer Valdemar Poulsen invented the tape recorder.

1932 Walt Disney released the first color cartoon.

1950's Researchers in the United States developed acrylic paints.

1958 Stereo records and players were invented.

1975 The first filmless camera was developed.

1982 Audio CD's were released in Japan and Germany.

2000 Most camera companies stopped making film cameras.

Glossary

acrylic a type of paint that is made with synthetic (human-made) chemicals.

amplifier; amplify a device for making audible the sounds recorded on a phonograph record or tape; to make greater or louder.

animation the preparation of an animated cartoon.

archaeologist a person who studies the people, customs, and life of ancient times.

assembly line a row of workers and machines along which work is passed until the final product is made.

broadcast (n.) something sent out by radio or television; a radio or television program of speech, music, or the like. (v.) to send out programs by radio or television.

camcorder a videocassette recorder combined with a color camera.

camera obscura a box or small chamber with a pinhole opening.

cassette a container that holds magnetic tape.

civilization nations and peoples that have reached advanced stages in social development.

commercial having to do with trade or business.

compact disc (CD) a round, flat platter on which recorded music, computer data, or other information is stored in the form of digital code.

daguerreotype an early type of photograph made on a metal plate, or the method of making such a photograph.

digital information that has been converted into a numeric code.

dry-plate process a process using a gelatin covered photographic plate for recording an image.

electric current the movement or flow of electric charges.

electric piano an electric musical instrument. An electric piano's sound is amplified through speakers.

electromagnet a piece of iron with a wire coiled around it. When an electric current passes through it, the iron becomes a strong magnet.

electronic of or having to do with electrons.

electronics devices that make use of electric power and transistors. Cellular telephones, computers, and televisions are examples of electronics.

emulsion a mixture of liquids where one liquid contains minute drops of the other liquid evenly throughout it.

engineer a person who invents, plans, or builds things, such as engines, machines, bridges, or buildings.

exposure the time taken to record an image on a photographic plate or film.

film a roll or sheet of thin, flexible material with a coating that is changed by light, used to take photographs.

fine arts the arts depending upon taste and appealing to the sense of beauty.

fix to set a photographic image with chemicals so that it will not fade.

frame one of the individual pictures on a strip of motion-picture film.

fresco the act or art of painting with water colors on the damp, fresh plaster of a wall or ceiling.

hammer one of the padded mallets for striking the strings of a piano.

hammered dulcimer a stringed musical instrument. The strings stretch over a four-sided sounding board.

harpsichord a stringed musical instrument like a piano. The sound comes from plucking the strings with a piece of leather or a quill instead of striking them with a hammer.

Hollywood the American motion-picture industry.

immigrant a person who comes into a foreign country or region to live.

Impressionism a style of painting that gives the impression made by the subject on the artist without much attention to details. Impressionism was developed by French painters of the late 1800's.

industry any branch of business, trade, or manufacture.

Internet a vast network of computers that connects many of the world's businesses, institutions, and individuals.

laser a device that produces an intense, focused beam of light.

motion picture a series of pictures on a strip of film recording very slight changes in position of persons or things, and projected on a screen at such a speed that the viewer gets the impression that the things pictured are moving.

mural a picture painted on a wall.

negative a photographic image in which the lights and shadows are reversed.

organ a musical instrument made of pipes of different lengths, which are sounded by compressed air blown by a bellows, and played by keys arranged in one or more keyboards.

palette knife a thin, flexible knife that is used for mixing colors and as a painting tool.

patent to get a government-issued document that grants an inventor exclusive rights to an invention for a limited time.

phonograph an instrument that reproduces the sounds from records.

photography recording an image by exposing it to a light-sensitive film or plate.

piano a stringed instrument that is played by depressing keys that cause padded hammers to strike the strings, which produce sounds.

pigment a coloring material, usually a powder. When pigments are mixed with oil, water, or some other liquid, it makes paint.

portable media player a handheld device used for listening to music or spoken word, or for watching videos.

project to cause an image to fall on a surface or into space.

projectionist a person who runs a motion picture projector.

projector a device for projecting an image on a screen.

Renaissance a great cultural movement that began in Italy during the early 1300's.

Roman of or having to do with ancient Rome or its people. The Roman Empire controlled most of Europe and the Middle East from 27 B.C. to A.D. 476.

solvent a liquid that can dissolve other substances.

soundboard a thin, resonant piece of wood that increases the fullness of the tone of a musical instrument.

sound track a recording of the sounds of words, music, and action, made along one edge of a motion-picture film.

sound waves a wave produced by the vibration of an object.

still camera a device for taking photographs.

synthesizer an electronic instrument, usually played with a keyboard, that produces sounds like various other instruments.

synthetic human-made.

tape recorder a machine that records sounds or other electrical signals magnetically on plastic tape and plays them back.

telegraph an instrument used to send messages by means of wires and electric current.

wet-plate process a process that coats a glass plate with collodion to make it light-sensitive so it can be used for photographs.

Additional Resources

Books:

- *The Art Book for Children* by the editors of Phaidon Press (Phaidon Press, 2007).

- *Amazing Leonardo da Vinci Inventions You Can Build Yourself* by Maxine Anderson (Nomad Press, 2006).

- *Cave Paintings to Picasso* by Henry M. Sayre (Chronicle, 2004).

- *Dynamic Art Projects for Children* by Denise M. Logan (Crystal Productions, 2005).

- *Great Inventions : The Illustrated Science Encyclopedia* by Peter Harrison, Chris Oxlade, and Stephen Bennington (Southwater Publishing, 2001).

- *Great Inventions of the 20th Century* by Peter Jedicke (Chelsea House Publications, 2007).

- *The History of the Camera* by Elizabeth Raum (Heinemann Library, 2008).

- *Leonardo, Beautiful Dreamer* by Robert Byrd (Dutton, 2003).

- *So You Want to Be an Inventor?* By Judith St. George (Philomel Books, 2002).

- *What a Great Idea! Inventions that Changed the World* by Stephen M. Tomecek (Scholastic, 2003).

Web Sites:

- Art Games
  http://www.kids.albrightknox.org
  This Web site, maintained by the Albright-Knox Art Gallery in Buffalo, New York, contains a variety of fun learning activities for grades K-6.

- History, Arts, and Culture
  http://www.usa.gov/Citizen/Topics/History.shtml
  Official information and services from the U.S. government. Includes links to museums, libraries, and historical Web sites within the United States.

- Metropolitan Museum of Art: Explore and Learn
  http://www.metmuseum.org/explore/index.asp
  Explore the New York Metropolitan Museum of Art's artistic collection, read about artists, and learn more about cultures around the world on this useful Web site for students.

- National Gallery of Art (London): Kids Page
  http://www.nga.gov/kids/kids.htm
  Contains a wealth of activities and projects for students.

- The Renaissance Connection
  http://www.renaissanceconnection.org
  Learn all about inventions and artists from the Renaissance on Allentown Art Museum's interactive educational Web site.

- Thomas Alva Edison
  http://www.invent.org/hall_of_fame/50.html
  A Web site with biographical information on Thomas Edison.

- Timeline of Art History
  www.metmuseum.org/toah/splash.htm
  The Metropolitan Museum of Art displays objects from their collections in geographical and chronological context.

▶ Index

A
acrylic paint, 28-29
animation, 38-39
Archer, Frederick S., 34
Aristotle, 30-31
Armat, Thomas, 37
arts, 4-5

B
Babcock, Alpheus, 12
Bach, Johann Sebastian, 7, 11
Bell, Alexander Graham, 16
Berliner, Emile, 19
Brady, Mathew, 33
Bray, John Randolph, 38

C
camcorder, 37, 42
camera, 32-33; digital, 33, 42-43; motion-picture, 36-37, 40-42
camera obscura, 30-32
cassette, 19, 21, 23
CD. *See* compact disc
clavichord, 11
compact disc, 17, 19, 21-23
computer, 39, 42
Cristofori, Bartolomeo, 12
Ctesibius, 6

D
Daguerre, Louis, 32, 33
daguerreotype, 32-34
digital: camera, 33, 42-43; piano, 15; recording, 21-23
Disney, Walt, 39, 41
dry-plate process, 34-35
dulcimer: hammered, 8-9; mountain, 9

E
Eastman, George, 35
Eastman Kodak Company, 35, 42
Edison, Thomas, 18, 36, 37
electronic keyboard, 14-15
electronic organ, 7

F
Fantasia (film), 41
film, 32, 34-35, 43; motion picture, 36, 38, 40, 41
fine arts, 4
Fox Talbot, William Henry, 33
fresco, 28

G
Greece, ancient, 6, 24, 30-31

H
hammer, 8-10, 12, 14
Hammond, Laurens, 7
harpsichord, 10-11; piano replacing, 11-13
Hoxie, Charles A., 40
Hurd, Earl, 38-39
hydraulis, 6

I
Impressionism, 27
Internet, 23, 43
invention, 4

J
Jazz Singer, The (film), 40

K
keyboard instrument: dulcimer, 8-9; electronic keyboard, 14-15; organ, 6-7. *See also* harpsichord; piano
kinetoscope, 36-37
Kodak camera, 35

L
laser, 23
Leonardo da Vinci, 26
Lumière brothers, 37

M
Maddox, Richard L., 34
magnetic tape, 20-21
microphone, 16-17
Mo Di, 30
Morales, Rodolfo, 4
motion picture, 5, 17, 30, 36-37; animated, 38-39; sound track, 40-41
mural, 28, 29
musical instrument, 4, 5. *See also* keyboard instrument
Muybridge, Eadweard, 36

N
negative, 33-35
Niépce, Joseph, 32

O
oil paint, 26-27
organ, 6-7
Orozco, José Clemente, 28

P
paint: acrylic, 28-29; oil, 26-27; tempera, 24-25
palette knife, 26
phenakistoscope, 38
phonograph, 18-19, 22
photography, 30; digital, 42-43; motion picture, 36-39; with camera, 32-33. *See also* film
piano, 7, 8, 12-13, 41; digital, 15; electric, 14-15; harpsichord replaced by, 10-13; player, 13
Plateau, Joseph Antoine, 38
portable media player, 23
Poulsen, Valdemar, 20

R
record. *See* phonograph
red carmine, 25
Rego, Paula, 29
Renaissance, 8-10, 25, 27, 28
Rhodes, Harold, 15
Rivera, Diego, 28, 29
Rome, ancient, 6, 24
Ruckers, Jan, 10
Russell, James T., 22-23

S
Sasson, Steven, 42
Scheele, Carl, 32
Schulze, Johann, 32
Scott de Martinville, Édouard-Léon, 19
Siqueiros, David, 28
Slim, Sunnyland, 14
sound track, 40-41
sound waves, 17-19
Steinway, Henry E., 12
synthesizer, 15

T
tape recorder, 20-21
telegraph, 16
telephone, 16
tempera paint, 24-25

V
van Eyck, Jan, 27
van Gogh, Vincent, 27

W
wet-plate process, 34
Wurlitzer piano, 14, 15